Walking with Buddha

(through love, loss and life)

Volumes 1, 2 & 3

A. P. RANSOME

WITH A FOREWORD
BY NAN WITCOMB
– AUTHOR OF
THE THOUGHTS OF NANUSHKA

BALBOA.
PRESS
A DIVISION OF HAY HOUSE

Balboa Press books may be ordered through booksellers or by contacting:

Balboa Press
A Division of Hay House
1663 Liberty Drive
Bloomington, IN 47403
www.balboapress.com.au
1 (877) 407-4847

ISBN: 978-1-4525-2790-1 (sc)
ISBN: 978-1-4525-2791-8 (e)

Print information available on the last page.

Balboa Press rev. date: 05/26/2015

Other references
www.philipransome.com.au including blog posts

To my little brother,
Rick

(May 1965 to September 2001—thirty-six short years)

~ Happy 50th Birthday Rick – 2015 ~

Contents

Foreword

By Nan Witcomb

Philip Ransome is a man with a poet's soul. He invites us into his heart which is filled with memories and his dreams of what might have been. He is not a Buddhist, but chose the title for his poems and thoughts, *Walking With Buddha (through Love, Loss and Life)* because similar beliefs brought him out of a very sad, bewildering world when he lost his dear brother, Rick, who tragically died unexpectedly at a very young age.

Philip bravely reveals his feelings at that time, and in the years which followed. He gives us an understanding of others who have lost loved ones, but more importantly how it can affect many of us in the same way.

One of the lesser known results of these tragedies in our lives can bring confusion and a desperate yearning for love to fill our loneliness. With incredible honesty, Philip tells us of many loves which have now become memories and his dreams of what might have been.

His descriptions of the breath-taking moment when we begin to fall in love, will appeal to young and old and men and women. Philip travelled the world, became a proud and loving father and moved on to become a successful business advisor with a poet's soul that he is today.

You will be surprised at how many of his thoughts are also yours.

Nan Witcomb
nanushka@senet.com.au

Acknowledgements

My appreciation to Bridget for all your love and support as this book of volumes has been put together, and for all we have been through together. For my boys, William and Jack, who have endured my endless keystrokes and my many ups and downs. I have learnt so much from you both. For Annette Rohde, for the coffee and important advice about the initial style — my thanks for your direction and guidance. To Marilyn Mayne, a fine artist whose works adorn these pages. Thanks Marilyn also for your support of the arts in South Australia and in Port Lincoln. To Sophie Panagopoulos, thank you for your unique sketches. To those that sketch and paint, continue to stretch your creative souls. They are sought after in a modern world.

And to Nan (Nan Witcomb), without your inspiration and guidance and picking up that initial copy of the *Thoughts of Nanushka* many years ago, I have to say a big thank-you for your honesty but also for what has become a good friendship. You have inspired many people around the world including myself and I truly appreciate what you have given the literary world. Many thanks.

Author's Note

Let me take you back to a moment in time - it is September 11, 2001.

I am writing the eulogy for Rick, my brother who is two years younger than me, who had passed away a few days earlier at my mother's home. The world for me stopped from the moment I received a call saying there was something wrong with Rick. I drove there in a panic and raced in.

'What do you think is wrong?', Mum asked.

I literally yelled back, 'Mum, he's dead. Call emergency!'

I pulled him to the floor, chest and head up. In between breaths into his mouth and pushing on his chest, I shouted to Mum, 'It's triple zero. Dial triple zero. Breathe, Rick. Come on, breathe..' I wondered how long he had already been like this. Was it a few minutes? Was it more?

I looked upward. I believed there was some God but was not sure, and I cried out, 'I can do anything, but why won't you let me revive him?' I started crying, finding it hard to breathe myself. Again and again, I breathed into his mouth, pushed in his chest to get a breath, and listened to what Mum was telling me the ambulance was saying on the phone. I looked up again. I only had one wish right now. 'God, why can't you hear me?' The next minute I was watching the ambulance officers push adrenaline into Rick's arms, shot after shot. No response. My sister, Vicki, had arrived and was looking after Mum. Eventually they pronounced Rick dead, and for someone who always had a direction and a purpose, I was suddenly lost.

Now I was in my living room, trying to put words to Rick's character, trying to make sense of his short thirty-six years. I looked up at the television. A plane had just hit one of the Twin Towers in New York. It was early morning there. Minutes later the second tower was hit, and I watched the coverage in disbelief. Was the world falling apart? What would Rick say? He was the journalist, the writer in the family. I called my wife and my brother to the room. We watched as the towers fell. My wife tried to call her cousin, who lived in Clifton, New Jersey. Were they working in New York on this day? No connections were available. It was a disastrous day for humanity.

I used to love to see the light of day, but now I failed to see the point of work, of family, and of life. When I drank, I drank longer and harder and was more confused. Through this, though, I did one good thing.

I managed to produce a book titled *My Life Slipped through My Fingers*, a book that I hope paid testimony to Rick's creative and intellectual abilities. The book not only showcased his talents but also gave something to his family, his friends, and me. We have a little piece of him to remember and can re-live his sorrows and his triumphs, know his joys and what would upset him. More importantly his work will not remain in a box on a shelf or in a cupboard. Production of the book gave me some time to breathe, and for the better part, I thought it would put my grief to rest and my loss at some sort of ease for brief moments.

I have no religious persuasion or background, and this, my second book, is not a book on Buddhism per se. If you can imagine for a moment someone who is supportive of all your inconsistencies; tolerant of all your changes in moods; wise enough to be able to give advice when you have needed it, even when you didn't need to hear it; challenging you to think beyond where you are now present; and caring enough to ask how you are and not tell you how he is and to listen without criticism or prejudice; loving enough to understand your ups and downs and then someone who can help you through the mental anguish of letting go or understanding, then for me, that represents a 'Buddha' moment. A time when you feel you are in the hands of someone with all those great capabilities to assist you to move toward the next important level in your life. The concept of Buddha has been important for me to understand my inner self. My Buddha has given me the welcoming hand of strength to go from day to day, when on some occasions I would have found it easier to give my own life away. Others may find their own Buddha that gives them the internal strength to believe in themselves, to believe and comprehend a meaning to their life, and more importantly to believe in the need to move on.

Often when we lose someone, the pain we feel shows in our expressions and feelings and manifests sometimes as anger and depression, a feeling of 'wanting out,' loss of caring, a loss of being able to communicate properly, or behaviours that aren't what others would call normal. In my case, I often found I couldn't breathe, let alone communicate to all the people around me, for what seemed an eternity. On some days, amidst the pressures of family, life, work, and love, I have wondered why it was not me who died on that fateful September day in my mother's lounge room.

I've thought that this is my own personal hell, re-living that September day again and again. Moving on is never easy, and as many times as we are offered help, for many of us it is something we struggle to accept, especially without that other person nearby. During this time, I wanted to consult someone, a friend or a colleague, but didn't have the internal strength to take the first step. This is where *Walking with Buddha* started. *Walking with Buddha* is my journey.

Importantly, I didn't want to write something that focused on the gloomy times; rather, I wanted to write something that embodied all the things in life, including emotions, funny and serious contemplations, philosophy, and above all, a touch of fiction. I hope you enjoy the journey, one that you can reflect upon. Open a page and discover something about life, about that Buddha in you, as I have. May your Buddha hold your hand through life and give you the guidance and patience you deserve. May your soul recover from that inner point where all appears lost. May you be at peace with the world and with yourself and may you continue your journey as I am.

—A. P. Ransome.

Somebody should tell us, right at the start of our lives,
that we are dying.
Then we might live life to the limit,
every minute of every day.

—Michael Landon

Volume 1

BECOMING

I had never considered not seeing you again,
not holding your hand,
not smelling that sweet scent you wear,
nor considered not feeling the rush of excitement
at the touch of your lips
or the sound of your voice.

I had not considered knowing
who you might have in your arms tonight.
I hold my breath waiting to see you again,
wondering if you still feel the same way
as when we first spent time together,
…the night we met.

The autumn leaves have fallen - I think of you today,
my yesterdays remind me of where my thoughts might be,
about what was a broken moment
in a street so far away?
My smiles and memories of a love are what I see.

When winter comes and warmth is still within my heart,
rekindling those memories of when it all began,
And what I could have held in dreams each night
right from the start?
Instead I wonder almost every night if I
am that same man...

Years have passed since we first met,
I fell in love without meaning to.
My dreams were rich, I'll not forget,
their colours glassed in dew.

Wanted to hold you in my arms each night
and feel your warmth from year to year,
buy you things that felt just right,
to conjure up those happy tears.

Wanted to miss you when you went away
but still feel your warmth inside my heart,
to keep those memories of love alive,
and perhaps we'd never part.

Smile

A shower of mid-morning sunlight
pours through the window
of winter.

Crispy leaves
break under footprints.

Rain patters on my roof.
The gentle thumping,
like a comforting smile.

Summer nights,
steaming waters.
A warm breeze.

Thoughtful hello,
memories shared
from youthful past.

A moonlit bay,
discovering new moments
and warmth within.

Changing colour
before falling,
my leaves of life.

Scented paper,
timeless seasons
in your words.

Crowded bookshelf,
a yesterday filled
with memories.

Cheerful photographs,
tracing back
past loves.

One missing photo,
something unseen
but remembered.

I feel the spark of new love
as my cheek graces yours,
sense your warm embrace
before we touch.

I swim in dreams of you
hoping never to wake.

I live for your smile
and the music of your love.

They share a gift of love,
a sign they really care.
Once more, his lips go to hers.
He holds her at his side,
gently whispering kind reminders
of the future which lies ahead.
At peace and never anxious
about what their future holds.
Love will always be there,
as long as that love unfolds.

Walk with Purpose

He was broken hearted
when she said her last good-byes.
Inside him, something had gone,
he felt empty, something had died.
'Was it only physical?'
but hadn't he always given her
so much more?
Perhaps it was those eyes,
charm or the warmth of her smile.
He would be so very sad when she had gone
probably in tears,
missing that one moment
when their caring
had made it so much more than physical.
That's what breaks his heart.

*I've been away
such a long time
and missed your love.*

I can feel you near me,
a shudder as our arms touch,
almost electric.

Waiting in anticipation
for what this moment holds…

Our breathing synchronised,
while you lie here beside me...

but for a moment.

You walk beside me,
   faithful,
      sorrowful eyes looking up,
      you walk beside me,
         never expecting anything
            but companionship, love,
            and a pat.

All I hear
is your gentle breathing.
All I feel
is your soft touch.
Your longing and desire
surround me.

All I smell
is your perfume.
Your secrets lie with me.

All I want
is to dream with you.
To touch and feel
and listen
… to your whisper.

Pink shoes sit in a corner,
pink socks sitting beside.
pink bodies lying together,
their love has nothing to hide.

Blue jeans folded on the floor,
blue songs don't make them blue.
'Blue Boy' looks down from his portrait,
at a dream that's about to come true.

The soft feathered quilt surrounds him
as she attends to a need,
love shedding light to a darkness,
away from a world without creed.

All loneliness has left them,
eyes remain closed as they kiss.
Two strangers, two lovers together,
away from the world and in bliss.

I look inside for your soul,
for the whole of you,
for everything that you are
which I cannot see
with just a glance.

I sit on the edge of your bed,
although you are lying there beside me,
I feel I'm alone in the room.
What time is it...
and where have the hours gone?

Sitting here, talking until two,
wondering just what you see in me.

Whether you know those times
when I might seem far away,
I am so close to your heart.

On the edge of your bed,
dreaming.

I can't stop the way I feel inside.
Why does my heart still bleed?

Sharing memories
with someone so far away.

Loving the scent
which takes me to a place
where I can feel again.

There are no secrets,
there is no other.
I take the time to wonder
just where it all began.

Take my hug, if you need to feel my embrace,
and the warmth of someone close.
Talk to me if you need to
share the pain of what you know,
or don't know.

There are times when we don't move on,
when we need to,
when we can't give up
what we once had and shared,
but we have to.

When we fail to see how it could get worse
or when it will be better,
it's always a struggle to let go,
when things seem somehow comfortable,
when we care about someone so much -
we have to take that first bold step
and move on.

*It's not what they see
in who we are*

*but just being
who we are*

The small snowflakes in the air
remind me of that embrace I will never forget
and always desire.

Our cheeks touching as we hold each other close....

In the cold of winter,
a fire burns inside.

Against a sky full of stars,
occasionally touching hands,
bottle of wine between us.
Allowing the red to breathe,
we share a crystal chalice.

As we sit reminiscing about life and love,
about a friendship which has allowed us
to sometimes touch hands -
through our meandering lives.

The voice of James Blunt
comes floating up to us,
I close my eyes for a moment,
open them to find you looking at me,
you are smiling at what we share.
We sit closer together again.
James, the sky is bringing your voice up to us.
We close our eyes and breathe
           from within our crystal chalice.

I have walked on the beach alone,
felt the waters run through my toes
and sand wash over my feet.
I wondered where you were
and who you walked with.

She closes her eyes
and in that instant
goes somewhere deep within herself
where no one can touch her -
A place where she is dreaming
of all the pleasures she has had
and those which have passed her by.
She tries not to open her heart
to the world again.

Sometimes I try to find
that photograph we shared.

Looking through the suitcase
with all the memorabilia
which I keep tucked away,
finding letters that make me smile
as I read every line.

It doesn't hurt anymore,
even when I read about you in the papers
or hear your voice on radio.

Everything is better now
I have moved on.

Volume 2

At One Time

Forever my beating heart

I smiled at a picture of us holding hands.

Remember when we were kids
listening to the television
we would hear,

*'When you wish upon a star,
makes no difference who you are.'*

It was at that time
when we could dream anything,
be anyone and conquer all.
Everything was achievable
when we were kids.
Wasn't it?

Sun's rays
lighten the morning,
waking.

Frosty window,
your reflection,
only a reminder.

Soft kiss,
music reaching
my heart.

The heart,
warming to love,
I smile.

Dancing
Silent whispers
Longing to touch.

Rain patters
on my window.
Are you coming?

We have withdrawn from the city to country
to be closer to nature and friends,
to get back to our roots
and to breathe in that pure country air again.

Although we knew it long ago,
we'd forgotten how the life had fast consumed us.

We need a reminder of what it means
to live among family and friends,
replacing the fast life with pure country air,
more room to move and some peace in the end.

Although we knew it long ago,
we have discovered who we were.

Don't have regrets.

This time last year I made apricot jam.
I ventured out in our warmest months
to see what the heat had in store on the tree.
Clumped on branches that sagged,
was it the weight of purple plums that
made it easy for me to pick them?

All around were the bobs of plastic and silver
to distract the birds.
I need to scare them away;
I don't want them to feast.
Leave me some plums
so I might have some jam.

Take the apples or strawberries
or fruit up the hill
of a neighbour who couldn't care less
to protect their fruit from the birds
that now call
saying the plums are ripe for picking.

Satsuma, Satsuma—tightened and crisp,
ripened in our hottest months,
beckoning me to start cleaning some jars
so I might have some jam.

There was that tap, tap, tap on the roof.
The tin roof was too shallow
and maybe there was no insulation.
Dad used to say you could smell the crispness in the air
before it rained.
It would spatter on the roof first,
until it changed from a tap
to a crescendo of water
hitting the empty drains.

Mum never liked the wet or the cold,
and that tap, tap, tap held her prisoner.
She sat inside, with the rugs and blankets
pulled up high around her.
It kept everything out
but the deafening noise of the rain.

Waiting for their footsteps
on the stairs.
It can't be much longer.
Birds start to twitter in the trees out there,
making more noise
than those anticipated footsteps.
Dawn breaks through the curtain
and I wait.
Five minutes, ten minutes,
soon I hear them.
Light footsteps on the stairs,
then silence -
where have they gone?
Then as if by miracle,
they stand beside me,
I hear them whisper,
'Dad, Father Christmas has been...
can we open our presents now?'

This year is the last time
that we will talk of Father Christmas.
The boys have asked questions
and must be wondering
why no one else believes in him.

I have to believe in the white-bearded man
who comes around midnight,
feeds his reindeer, checks his list for
who has been good or who has been bad,
leaves the presents
and takes flight to another home.

And it doesn't matter if we cannot see him.
In our hearts,
great things always happen
at Christmas.
Don't they?

My father, gone, not forgotten.
I have tried to keep you
from my heart.
One brother looks puzzled,
the other looks angry,
wondering who you were
and why you left without explaining.
My brothers won't tell me
and my mother won't talk about
just who you were.
Why?

The peace I see in your face
as you lie asleep in my arms,
is only surpassed by the joy
I see when you wake.

I treasure fatherhood
to such a degree,
that life without it
would mean little to me.

Before I go to bed,
I watch my babies sleep,
tuck them up nice and warm.
They look so happy
my heart warms too.

I slow my pace so he can keep up,
his hand reaches up to mine,
he clings to my thumb
and holds on tight,
knowing he is in a safer place.

Now he holds my hand.
I glance down to see his smile.
He looks up and breaks my heart as he asks.
'Will you be my dad?'

Holding my hand
as we cross the road.
There will come a time
when you've grown older and stronger,
you will choose your independence
over the security of your Dad's hand.
I can enjoy this for a little longer,
hoping you will plan
to do the same for your children
before they grow up
and cross the road on their own.

I know there is a distance between us
but all I need is a phone call or a text.
I so want you to be happy
in the place you call home.

Perhaps we should hold hands
and start again.

I can remember you, my love
and it makes me smile –
long ago I was part of your life
for a little while.

Our friendship today,
makes me smile
Because it's based on being part of your life,
long ago...
for a little while.

All in a moment,
he glances across the road, looks her up and down,
seemingly takes forever
to digest the colour of her skin.
She has a freshness in her face, a smile,
she dresses well.
She has auburn hair,
a gentle curl that sweeps in front of her shoulders,
and she doesn't mind showing cleavage?
Why not? It's her life, after all.
She is confident and looks good, so why not show it?
She can.
Her legs are long.
God, she must be all of five foot ten or more.
Taller in those shoes.
She must be mid-thirties?

Then he turns his stare away
as he notices me,
        walking beside her.

We made the phone call last night.
Distance has claimed
another friendship.
Although we talked,
something has changed,
we have grown apart.

You have hurt my heart
and what is left is torn,
my light has turned to dark.

I miss you and go to places we used to go,
walk the same paths,
tread the same steps,
and kid myself,
somehow, I will see you there.

Where were you when I called?
The distance makes me desperate
I need to hear your voice.
I try again,
but there is no answer,
wonder where all the time has gone
while you're so far away.

*There is nothing
without passion,
nothing without spirit,
nothing without learning,
except growing.*

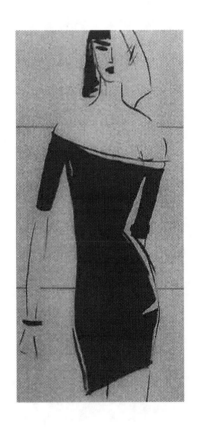

I wish I could promise
to be forever in your life
but I know in my heart
you are someone else's wife.
You have played with my heart
and would do this all again.
I would hold you in my arms
but I can't
share my love again.

You posted me on your site,
you didn't ask me,
worse still,
tagged in an embarrassing moment
which you thought
was funny.

Then the World Wide Web
was consuming me,
capturing my identity,
my location, my face, my friends,
worse still,
my past,
…as I tried to leave it all behind.

Say yes,
for all that it means,
for all that it deserves,
for yourself.

You tell me in your 'proper' British voice -
'End of call.'
I know, I pushed the button, after all.
But you repeat it again to me,
as if somehow I have forgotten.

Thank you, I repeat back to the Bluetooth in my car.
I prefer your voice to that of the American lady.
She sounds a little plastic
whereas you sound calm,
good company for this drive.

End of call.
I know, again.

How can you sit there opposite me naked,
playing the violin, flaunting yourself?
No one has listened to you play naked, bar myself.
Your auburn hair lies still,
falling around the waist of the violin.
Your legs are crossed,
naked in front of me.

Your eyelids stay closed in this next chorus,
as if you are dreaming.
Locked away in another feast of music
oblivious to me,
because you are in a picture frame.
You hold the violin so eloquently
somewhere under
your cheek.
You sit there naked, playing in front of me.

Could have been the uniform
that made you so attractive,
shield near your left shoulder,
gold buttons on blue,
or the sweep of your hair.

Perhaps the hat you wore on the side
or the baton which lay at your waist.
I watched you every day
walk the same beat,
     just hoping to be booked.

Listen, Listen!
What?
Can't you hear it?
Can't I hear what?
Listen! Listen!
Like tiny bombs, crackling away
amidst all the other noise.
Listen! Listen!
You're not trying!
I bent over a little nearer,
opened my ears to the world
and heard the snap, crackle, and especially the pops
of Rice Bubbles.
His smile spread wider as he listened,
keeping his head down,
not too close to the milk
as his ear savoured the sound of each bubble,
until it had snapped, crackled and popped,
it's life gone, soaked up in milk.

I watch as they cut and toast some bread.
One cuts some onion to mix with the tuna,
a tear appears in his eye.

The toast is buttered, hot.
The onion mixed in with the tuna flakes
is smeared over the toast.

They both smile.
'This is the way Grandma made it, Dad.'

Was it only just a year ago?

Amidst the company of strangers
at another convention,
looking around and wondering why I am here.
Aside from margins and profits,
who is my shareholder?
How is my presence adding value
or making it easier
for others to live in peace,
free of politics and religion?

How am I making it a better place?
Without spending so much time
attuned to what the world needs
rather than what I need first?

How can I make it better for them
if it is not better for me?
*   So how do I get off this hurdy-gurdy?*

Looking blankly at each other,
why are they here having dinner,
physically but not emotionally?
Perhaps both are wondering
where it had all gone wrong?
Did she ever really care for him?
Did he ever really care for her?
Their thoughts could be identical.

'I am looking through you. Where did you go?
I thought I knew you. What did I know?'

The melody of the Beatles plays through her
as she starts to hum ever so quietly.

They have let themselves go.

They know they've lost each other-
their relationship is at its worst,
perhaps they both are wondering
who had left first?

The wine succumbs to the gentle
curve of the glass.
The mouth of the glass is wide
to accept a dark-bodied red.

The glass lets the wine breathe
and airs the barrel's flavour.
I swill the wine.
(I wouldn't tell anyone that I drink
it quickly sometimes)

So much wine, so little time,
I take another sip and breathe
…life.

I can smell the red wine from yesterday
in the stains on the long table.
The bottles now lay empty
and although the taste was sweet,
today my throat is dry.

Amidst friends of old we shared stories
pleasured each other's company
with anecdotes of life,
as we filled each glass
and remembered.

Volume 3

WITHIN THE LIGHT

If you had stayed,
things may have been different
for us all.
Wish I had taken that photo of you,
running near the water's edge
keeping it as a memory
to bring you back into my life.

If you had stayed,
there would have been no need to stifle
those feelings of our love,
and I would no longer have to dream
of seeing you where the river meets the sea,
waiting for a memory
to bring you back into my life.

I remember a time
when we talked in hidden places,
when we met in dark lanes,
dreaming of one day
being able to meet you
among friends
and not in secret.

Danced on New Year's Eve,
lied a little,
heart torn a little more,
what was shared between us is no more.

Lied a little,
need a little more,
for something to hold my heart together
when the music stops
and we can dance no more.

I laugh at our
chance meeting,
for moments of time
that we had.
I only wish
you could stay.
Distance is what
is keeping us apart.

I could hear God calling,
but knew it was too soon to go
without good-byes.

Heard the echo of God's call,
travelled the world,
watched the full moon lighting up the sky,
walked on the beaches
and felt the sun on my body.

God's echo grew...
it was still too soon to go -
without good-byes.
I laid open my heart to my friends
and my enemies.

The echo grew to a lament.
I was ready.

The heart
warms to love
and memories.

Falling
in winter snow,
a melting heart.

Holding hands
across a table,
heart aglow.

The music,
eyes meeting,
temptation.

The touch,
hearts beating
souls on fire.

Remembering
a love
that might have been.

*L*ooking back on my life,
recalling years which have passed,
some seemed to go so slowly,
others flew by too fast.
Used to think I had noticed
the places that I'd been
but often failed to remember
the world which I had seen.

Growing older and wiser,
I ran at a pace,
felt stronger and faster
than those in the race.
I gave myself time
to build 'me' on my past,
but looked in the mirror
and only found glass.

We wonder about life
and the things we have done,
we reflect on ourselves
and what we've become.
If we fail to remember
a place or a face,
know the rush to the line
     is not really a race.

Checked this morning,
the text on my phone.
It happened last night,
your number is back in my life again,
I'm wondering why?

I dreamed for you never to leave,
but when you had gone,
I tossed and I turned as I waited for your call,
for a text, or any message at all…

Memories flood back as your number and photo
unfold on my phone.

Are you back in my life again?

If only I could mend the way you feel
and stop the pain I made you feel inside.
If only I could fill your heart with kindness
or take you to a place where the pain would run and hide.

If only a smile could bring back yesterday
and my tears meant you'd never have to cry,
if sharing those feelings I so often hide,
would make you see my love was not a lie.

If only I could be alone with you —
if my hugs could warm your lonely heart,
I would hold your hand so tightly
we would somehow know
that we would never, ever drift apart.
If only…if only.

I'll stay out here till mosquitos bite
and redness fills the sky.
I'll stay till the lights come on
and I begin to die.
Around me, all is loneliness,
something missing,
nothing new.
a grieving life is lonely
when there's nothing left to do.

As Christmas chimes out loneliness,
when the pipes of peace sound sad,
there seems nothing to leave a reminder
of the friends who we once had.
So I'll stay out here till mosquitos bite
forlorn as our friendship ends
I'll stay here till the lights come on,
and we can start again.

I walk alone on this Spring day
imagining you hadn't gone away -
you were the closest in my life.

With gentle laugh and wine in hand,
a generous and kind hearted man -
a simple man of life.

Springtime has come again,
I look for that dear familiar face -
only to see a missing place,
at a dinner...
      without a life.

My only wish
was that time had been slower
to make your life
last longer.

Picked up my guitar tonight -
remembering all those things about you
that I loved.
Kind words in testimonies
make their way towards my heart…
but cannot bring you back.

I imagine you looking down upon us
from somewhere in a star filled sky,
understanding all the things we do,
whether they be right and wrong,
whether they be truth or lies.

Understanding what you'd been through,
somehow seems to make me more complete
and makes me so very proud of you.

As I play gently on my guitar,
the memory of your voice and laughter
seem very clear to me,
remembering the part you played
in the lives of friends and family.

Tonight, it seems we are not so far apart,
and as long as I live, will never forget
those gifts you gave us
     from your heart.

*We always wish
we had more time to say good-bye
and maybe if we could,
it would mean more.*

*But could we ever have said
all the things we needed to say
to fill the hole in our hearts?*

It rained the day you died,
leaving a weeping wound.

We will always love you.

I thank God for our time together,
for it outscores the pain
and the rain.

My life was put on hold
I had lost my kindred spirit,
gone with my smile
was the sound of the shouts and laughter
of a friend I felt I had known forever.

Looking at the forest, it seemed to become
darkened passages of fur pines stretching skyward.
No light passed through it,
no light came from it.
There was a coldness,
which made me wonder
what path you had taken,
who was looking after you,
but more, who would look after me
        as I grew older.

The suddenness of death is overwhelming,
it collapses the bravest heart,
shakes the most sturdy.

It has weakened my soul
and loosened my tears.
I'll miss you
> *more than I can say.*

I hold your cold hand
and touch your face.
You are pale and still.
These are my last moments with you
before your funeral tomorrow.
Can't stop my tears from falling into the coffin,
can't bring you back,
but it is the coldness I'll remember
as I leave you now,
wondering why you have gone?

Waiting so long for your call,
holding my breath,
wishing for the phone to ring,
longing just to hear your voice.
At last!
My senses seem filled
with your touch, your thoughts
and your dreams.
Never wanting it to end,
but knowing I'll be anxiously awaiting,
your next call.

When the twinkle in those fairy lights
have lost their glimmer
and you look around to see your plans
have fallen through,
do you ever recount the times
you've thought about me
and the many things a friend like me
could do?

When the glimmer of those fairy lights
has turned to darkness,
you could be lonely
and feel you still have many dreams
to share.
Then all you need to do is phone me
and know I'll keep this promise,
'I'll be there.'

Perhaps I could share some dreams with you,
might even make you smile,
even if the Christmas lights
are switched off
for a while.

I listened to my heart today
and noticed time had got away.
I'd failed to call you yet again
in my busyness of life.

It was your voice I missed so much,
but there was no time to keep in touch,
really miss your friendship too
in the busyness of life.

So listened to my heart today,
thought of you so far away,
found time to call my soul mate
in my busyness of life.

What will I do
when I cannot nestle
in the middle
of your back?

*Leaves falling,
a time for clearing.*

Walked outside into the still of night,
the stars are shining bright.
No sound is heard but birds in flight.

White ghost gums in the outline,
where peace on earth is well defined
in a world of a very different kind.

In the dark and still of night,
begin to wonder if I might
have life's creation in my sights?

*I do miss the Cheshire Cat
in me*

*I shouldn't have let
that important part of myself
slip away.*

I saw them dancing,
twirling in the dim light
of a room laid bare of memories.

I smiled as they swung each other
round the floor,
gazing into each other's eyes,
dreams holding dreams
and remembered -

then the lights were turned off.

We could see small cracks
in their walls tonight,
all through the house.
Nothing was really said,
but more left unsaid,
glances at each other were cool,
smiling lips without smiling eyes.
Did we see a tiny crack?

Let's hope it can be sealed
before another of our friends
decide to go their separate ways
before the walls fall.

With my child's arms around me,
I remember yesterday
when I thought of myself first
and the future
was not as important
as it is now -

    that I have you.

'*Annabelle, stay where you are!*'
A cry came from afar.
'*Please don't move,*' *he pleaded,*
'*please don't move along the ledge.*
I'll promise things will be okay.
I'll never laugh. Please, dear God,
please just stay, please stay.
Don't move any closer to the edge.'

'*Damien, you don't love me now.*
You never did!
You took my love and wasted it.
Now there's nothing I can ever give.
So why come closer to me now?'
she cried the question out somehow
'*Why now?*' *she cried...*
and took her life
        and his.

Against the city back-drop,
sipping wine, smiling, laughing,
remembering good times
and reassuring you
that things will get better.
Realising what a friendship we have
and what holding your hand is worth.

We sat on the roof,
gazed out over the city,
reminding ourselves,
we were still young.

Holding each other close,
temptation,
I love the lingering feel
of your kiss,
the smile on your face,
seems to last forever.

Some days I find it hard,
to come to terms with my loss
and what it means.
Tears well in my eyes,
memories come flooding back,
pulling at the strings of my heart.

Remembering your laughter,
your kindness and generosity.

Re-living our childhood
again and again.
Seems as if it was only yesterday
you were here,
thinking about making life
better for each other
and the world.

I swear I saw the angel
from the corner of my eye,
not sure whether he was keeping an eye on me
or asking me to keep an eye on the people
I was with.

Were my eyes playing tricks on me, as we know they can?
Or was I to assume he may be trying to tell me
to be mindful of the steps ahead?

Do not mourn if I should pass,
I have made every moment last,
climbed the highest pinnacles,
flown through the sky,
played my favourite music,
reasoned till I cried.
Have travelled to many other lands,
embraced the cultures there,
where the poor must beg to live,
while the rich who rarely give,
walk by with noses in the air.

Whispering sincerest thoughts
and feeling love so often,
my hugs for friends and enemies
cause the hardest hearts to soften.
I have loved my children,
guided them through jungle and mountain pass.
Tried to be a diplomat,
with no bias for colour or class,
so having lived life to the full,
maybe touching your life in some small way,
do not mourn me should I pass,
    our spirits will surely meet again - some day.

Illustrations

1. Wednesday, December 5, 2012, Couple / Ζευγάρι, Sophie Panagopoulos
2. Wednesday, December 19, 2012, I see red / Τα βλέπω
3. Saturday, February 1, 2014, Arcades / Στοές, Sophie Panagopoulos
   κόκκινα, Sophie Panagopoulos
4. Mother and Child, Marilyn Mayne
5. Design school sketch (fashion designs), Marilyn Mayne
6. The Glass, Marilyn Mayne
7. Thursday, November 28, 2013, At the end of the pier /
   Στο τέρμα του μώλου, Sophie Panagopoulos
8. The Dancer, Marilyn Mayne
9. Tuesday, May 1, 2012, May day at the beach /
   Πρωτομαγιά στην παραλία, Sophie Panagopoulos

Original poems *'Do Not Mourn'*, *'A Walk in the Forest'*
and *'Watching the Forest'* first published in
My Life Slipped through My Fingers, 2003
(Privately published limited edition, South Australia)

'Two Lovers, Two Strangers' first published in
the 1987 Anthology of Australian Poetry,
William Cobbett Books, Sydney, Australia, 1987

'If' first published in Caress of the Moon,
The International Library of Poetry,
Joy Esterby, Editor, Australia Print Group,
Maryborough, Victoria, 1997

Other dedications and notes

Original poem, *'As Christmas Chimes Loneliness'* was dedicated to Charlie Price, a student at St Mark's residential college where I resided when studying. Charlie tragically took his own life a few days after I last saw him at the Queens Head Hotel in North Adelaide.

Original poem, *'A Walk in the Forest'* was dedicated to Gordon Johnson, an incredible friend and work colleague who died from cancer. At karaoke, he sang the English bits while I did the French bits of *'Michelle,'* by the Beatles.

Original poem, *'Plum Picking'* inspired by Robert Frost's *'After Apple Picking'*.

About the Author

A. P. Ransome was born and grew up in Port Lincoln, South Australia, before moving to Adelaide to study. Whilst at university, he resided at St Marks College in North Adelaide. He has continued to study and has travelled and experienced a lot of the world. He has held senior roles in a number of businesses and presently operates as a business advisor to many companies, locally and interstate. As a coach he offers advice to business leaders, managers, and many people who need an ear, someone to lean on, someone who will listen, and someone offering practical advice. He lives presently in Stirling in the Adelaide Hills, known for its village atmosphere and what he calls a little bit of England. He lives with his family and is an active contributor to the community through his not-for-profit organisations, Schools In Business and Speakers in Schools (www. schoolsinbusiness.org.au and www.speakersinschools. com.au).

About the Illustrators

Marilyn Mayne was educated at Walford House School in Adelaide and studied art at the South Australian School of Arts. She worked as a commercial artist for the Myer Emporium and for advertising agencies, including freelance commercial work. She moved to Port Lincoln in 1959 and there established a gallery and studio for her own work and the work of other local artists. She is highly commended and awarded. Her gallery is on King Street Port Lincoln (http://eyrearts.com/marilyn-mayne.html).

Sophie Panagopoulos lives in Patras, Greece, where she started an art blog (http://sophie-illustrates.blogspot.gr/). Sophie has lived in a number of countries around the world, including Australia. She looks for inspiration in finding beauty in what others see as mundane. Everything she posts on her blog represents a place she's been to, an object she's owned, or a person she found striking or who simply sat still long enough. Between 2008 and 2011 she attended drawing classes with local artists. She likes to use drawing to connect with the place that she's in and ponder over its history, the way people live, and how people's everyday routines, thoughts, fears, and joys determine space and vice versa, giving cities a living soul.

About Nan Witcomb

Nan Witcomb is known in Australia for her 'Thoughts of Nanushka' poetry. She lives in South Australia having retired from an extraordinary working life which began in a bank when she was fifteen years old. She became a nursing sister at 22, followed by some years as a flight hostess with Ansett Airlines where she became Senior Regional Hostess in South Australia. It was at this time, she self published her first 'Nanushka' book, 'Yesterday, Today and Tomorrow' Volume I. After 23 years with the airline, Nan managed a lovely little restaurant in a wine region for seven years after which she became a personality on a high rating local radio programme. All the time she was writing her 'Nanushka' thoughts. Her books are now in three beautifully bound hard covers - Volumes i – vi (1-6), volumes vii – xii (7-12) and volumes xiii – xviii (13-18). They are no longer in stores and Volumes i – vi (1-6) is out of print, however, Nan has limited numbers of volumes vii – xii (7-12) and volumes xiii – xviii (13-18) available. Her other books are 'Up Here and Down There' and 'In My Day' (or 'You and Me Before TV'). Nan believes Nanushka could live within each of us, belongs to everyone and yet to no-one. Perhaps Nanushka is a part of you. To contact Nan, email her at nanushka@senet.com.au.

Printed in the United States
By Bookmasters